PARTNERS

Created and Produced by Firecrest Books Ltd
in association with John Francis/Bernard Thornton Artists

Copyright © 2000 Firecrest Books Ltd
and Copyright © 2000 John Francis/Bernard Thornton Artists

Published by Tangerine Press™, an imprint of Scholastic Inc.
555 Broadway, New York, NY 10012

Tangerine Press™ and associated logo and design are trademarks of Scholastic Inc.

ISBN 0-439-20658-8

Printed and bound in Belgium
First printing, September 2000

P A R T N E R S

Bernard Stonehouse

Illustrated by
John Francis

TANGERINE PRESS™ and associated logo
and design are trademarks of Scholastic Inc.

For Heather

Art and Editorial Direction by
Peter Sackett

Designed by
Paul Richards, Designers & Partners

Edited by
Norman Barrett

Color separation by
**Sang Choy International Pte. Ltd.
Singapore**

Printed and bound by
Casterman, Belgium

—— Contents ——

Introduction	6
Ostriches and zebras	8
Cleaner-wrasse and coral cod	10
Oxpeckers and rhinoceroses	12
Honeyguides and honey badgers	14
False scorpions and longhorn beetles	16
Sooty shearwaters and tuataras	18
Ospreys and night-herons	20
Rufous kookaburras and termites	22
Striped remoras and white sharks	24
Galápagos red crabs and marine iguanas	26
Large blue butterflies and ants	28
Carmine bee-caters and Kori bustards	30
Egyptian coursers and Nile crocodiles	32
Gray hornbills and green monkeys	34
Pea-crabs and blue mussels	36
Cattle egrets and cape buffaloes	38
Shrimp fish and sea urchins	40
Shepherd fish and Portuguese men-of-war	42
Black garden ants and rose aphids	44
Black-capped chickadees and humans	46
Index	48

Introduction

Most animals make their own way through the world. Some can count on help from others of their own kind. Lions hunt together, deer and antelope run in herds to protect themselves against predators, and gulls fly together in flocks to increase their chances of finding food. Just a few form partnerships with other kinds of animals. These are the ones you will find in this book.

There are many different kinds of partnerships, but they are never just the result of casual meetings. Some animals, like ostriches and zebras, live successfully without each other, but often come together because they share the same areas and dangers. Others, such as oxpeckers and shepherd fish, are seldom found alone. They are more successful when they live with their respective hosts.

In some partnerships we see – or think we see – quite clearly how both species benefit. Honeyguides lead honey badgers to bees' nests, and feed when the badgers have opened the nests. In other cases it is not so clear. Pea-crabs are probably much safer within mussels than outside, but do the mussels gain anything from the deal? There is no reason to think that partners always benefit equally, although we still have much to learn about how some of these partnerships work.

Ostriches and zebras

On the wide plains of Africa live many kinds of grazing and browsing animals, ranging in size from tiny antelopes to elephants and giraffes. Grazers eat mainly grass. Browsers eat shoots and leaves from shrubs and bushes. Usually they live in groups – flocks or herds of a few dozen or more. You seldom find one on its own. This is because there are predators around – lions, hyenas, cheetahs, and other hunters that live by killing and eating them. On its own, one zebra, one antelope, even one baby elephant, could easily be caught by the killers. Each individual is safer within a group.

Sometimes the herds come together to form huge mixed groups, with hundreds of animals grazing and browsing together. Often a herd of zebras meets a flock of ostriches and the two team up, feeding and moving together. While they are feeding, both keep their heads down, concentrating hard on finding the right stems of grass or leaves. The ostriches are probably safer by having the zebras around, while the zebras gain an early warning system. Watching for predators, zebras see far across the plains, but ostriches stand taller and see farther. When the ostriches become frightened and decide to move on, the zebras move with them.

Cleaner-wrasse and coral cod

Several kinds of small fish that live near the seabed take up what may seem to be a strange and dangerous way of life. Called "barber-fish," they clean the surface of other fish, scraping off parasites, loose skin, and bacteria. Why barber-fish? Because they remind us of human barbers, who groom and clean up their customers – to the benefit of both.

Here, a cleaner-wrasse is cleaning the mouth of a much larger fish, a coral cod. There are about 600 different species (kinds) of wrasse, many of them highly colored and decorated with bands of blue, green, or pink. Most are predators, with razor-sharp teeth for cutting and biting. The bigger ones, including some up to 10 feet (3 m) long, browse on coral reefs and rocks, snapping up crabs and other small animals. It is an easy step for some of the smaller species of wrasse to browse on other fish, snapping up and eating the parasites, dead skin, and bacteria-infested mucus that cover their surface – even dodging, like this one, among the teeth and gills of the larger fish.

Barber-fish are never short of customers. Their hosts benefit greatly from regular cleaning, and may indeed depend on it to keep them free from parasites and disease.

— Oxpeckers and rhinoceroses

Oxpeckers are little birds of the starling family that live in small flocks on the African plains. They are brown or gray on their upper surface, white below, and have large bills, sharp curved claws, and stiffly feathered tails. There are two closely related species, red-billed and yellow-billed, both with huge golden-yellow eyes. Europeans farming in Africa years ago saw them perching on their oxen, seeming to peck them hard, and they gave these birds their common name. Oxpeckers also cling to many other kinds of mammals, from antelopes to rhinoceroses, like this one, pecking at ticks and other skin parasites, and snapping up biting flies that swarm about their hosts.

It is quite normal for a dozen oxpeckers to perch on one animal, trotting swiftly over its surface, clinging tightly to the skin as their host walks or runs. Stand still for a few minutes when a flock of oxpeckers is around, and they may well come and settle on you. When alarmed, they give a shrill call, alerting one another, and possibly their hosts, to danger.

Oxpeckers remove unwanted parasites, keep flies away, and clean wounds, all of which are sources of food. Sometimes their pecking opens up wounds, irritating and even damaging their hosts, who snap, shake angrily, and rub against trees to get rid of them.

Honeyguides and honey badgers

Honey, the sugary syrup that honeybees make from nectar, is a nourishing food welcome to many different kinds of animals. Bees use it to feed themselves and their maggotlike larvae (young), storing it in their nests in tiny wax cells. Often the nests are in hollow trees or cavities among rocks. A large bees' nest, containing several pounds of honey and young bees, is a good find for a hungry predator.

In the forests of Africa and Asia live small, compact black-and-gray mammals called honey badgers, or ratels. Like other kinds of badgers, they feed on a wide range of foods, including insects, berries, and snakes, and are fond of honey when they can find it. They tear into the nest with strong, sharp claws, while dense fur protects them from the stings of the angry bees.

In the trees nearby live small brown-and-white birds called honeyguides. They, too, are interested in bees' nests, not for the honey, but for the bees, larvae, and wax. When a honeyguide finds a nest, it seeks out a honey badger and gives a particular rattling call that attracts its attention. The bird then guides it to the nest, which the badger tears open, so both can feed.

— False scorpions and longhorn beetles

False scorpions, also called pseudoscorpions, are closely related to true scorpions but lack their stinging tail. About 1,600 different kinds live all over the world. Most are tiny, seldom more that a few tenths of an inch long, and are completely harmless to humans. Mainly carnivorous, they live under stones, in grass, in houses, even in libraries of old books, hunting and feeding on small insects.

Longhorn beetles get their name from their long antennae, which may be three or four times as long as the body. There are over 15,000 species, mostly tropical, some up to 6 inches (15 cm) long, others less than 1 inch (2.5 cm) long. They are flying insects, with wings that they tuck away under their brightly colored wing cases. Adults feed on pollen, while the larvae, or young, burrow in wood, feeding as they go. Some do serious damage to trees, others to buildings with wood frames.

False scorpions have no means of traveling except on their short legs, so they hitch rides on other animals. This longhorn beetle of central South America carries several false scorpions on its back and in its wing cases. They cause no trouble, and probably pay their way by feeding on mites and other parasites.

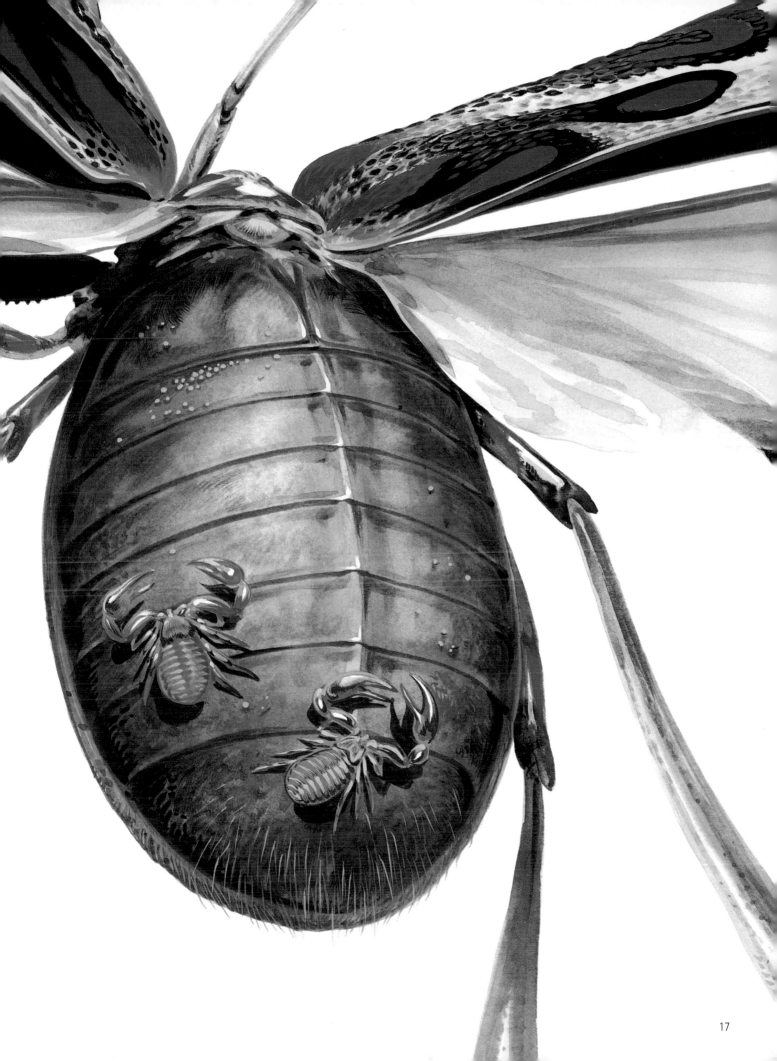

Sooty shearwaters and tuataras

Sooty shearwaters are seabirds that swoop and glide over the southern oceans in search of food. They have gray-brown plumage and long, slender wings, and nest in thousands on forested islands south of New Zealand and Australia. Each pair lays a single white egg, usually in a burrow 3 feet (1 m) or more long, scraped out of soft soil among the tree roots. Parents take turns to incubate the egg and brood the single chick that emerges.

Occasionally, a parent with a home on one of the New Zealand islands returns to find that a lodger has moved in and taken over the burrow. About 2 feet (60 cm) long, the intruder looks like a large lizard, but is in fact a tuatara, a kind of reptile that is now found only on these very few islands. Tuataras are not friendly lodgers. This one may already have eaten the egg or chick, and may be ready to defend the burrow against its rightful owner. Or it may just be resting in the entrance during daylight, ready to move off after nightfall to seek an unoccupied burrow for itself. Are they in partnership? It is hard to say. Perhaps they are just two animals in the same burrow.

Ospreys and night-herons

Among lakeside and seaside trees in coastal areas of the world, you sometimes see messy tangles of sticks, seaweed, and dried grasses. These are the nest platforms of the osprey, or fish-hawk. Ospreys, with 5-foot (1.5-m) wingspans, live by catching fish at the surface or in shallow waters. Hovering 100 feet (30 m) in the air to spot their prey, they plunge in spectacular dives, turning at the last moment to strike with their feet, grasping the fish in their sharp, curved talons.

When ospreys return in spring to their traditional breeding grounds, they spend the first few days bringing more sticks to their nest platforms, repairing the damage of winter storms. Then they pile up softer material in one corner to make a nest, laying three eggs that the females alone incubate. A big platform may be large enough for two nests, but a pair of ospreys would never allow other ospreys to build alongside their nest. However, they sometimes tolerate other species. Here, a night-heron, a long-legged bird that fishes along the banks of lakes and streams, shares the platform under the osprey nest, looking after her own three eggs. It seems to be a sensible, practical arrangement. Neither species threatens the other, and both may benefit by helping to keep gulls and other predators away from their nests.

Rufous kookaburras and termites

Rufous kookaburras are Australian kingfishers about 18 inches (45 cm) long, with a white or pale gray body, brown wings and tail, and a huge bill. "Rufous" means reddish-brown. "Kookaburra" echoes the crazy, laughing call of these birds. Once heard, you never forget it. You always know when kookaburras are around, particularly in the early mornings and late evenings when they are noisiest. Kookaburras feed on small animals, including birds and reptiles. They are renowned for killing snakes longer than themselves, which they grasp in their bills and batter to death on the ground.

Kookaburras nest in hollow trees, rock crevices, and mud banks, digging deeply to provide a safe cavern for their eggs and young. This pair has found a hole 10 feet (3 m) above the ground in the side of a termite's nest. They have enlarged the hole and burrowed into the chambers and walls of hardened mud so laboriously built and maintained by the termites. The birds are well protected from outside predators, and seem not to be worried by the insects within. Perhaps this is a part of the nest that the termites have abandoned. Kookaburras fiercely keep other animals away from their nest, so help to defend the termite nest against possible predators.

— Striped remoras and white sharks

The ocean is a dangerous place, full of snapping jaws and teeth, where small fish in particular are likely to get eaten. Among the predators, there are none more liable to be hungry than great white sharks. Swimming in front of a shark would be asking for trouble. Swimming behind it, or better still, hanging onto its underbelly, is much safer. The shark itself cannot see its passenger, and when there is a shark around, other predators will keep far away.

This is the way of life adopted by remoras, a strange kind of fish of the perch family that live in tropical seas. There are eight species, all distinguished by a ridged sucker on top of the head, by which they clamp themselves onto other fish and are pulled along through the water. They can hitch a ride, or cast off and swim freely on their own. Some kinds of remoras, just a few inches long, live inside the mouth or gill cavity of a host fish. This striped remora, almost 3 feet (90 cm) long, holds on to the outside of this great white shark. When the shark approaches a school of fish, the remora lets go and hunts for itself. After feeding, it latches on to another host, to hitch another oceanic ride.

Galápagos red crabs and marine iguanas

The Galápagos Islands, 600 miles (970 km) off the west coast of South America, are home to a strange collection of unusual animals, from giant tortoises to tropical penguins. Under constant equatorial sunshine, the islands tend to be dry and inhospitable, so many of the animals live close to the sea and feed in it. Among them are these iguanas – reptiles like giant lizards, over 6 feet (2 m) long with hard, scaly skin. They feed among the beds of seaweed growing around the islands. Between meals they bask on the shore, warming themselves and resting in the sun.

The red crabs also live along the shore, though lower down, in the splash zone where the waves keep them cool and damp. Scratching a living from the small plants and animals that cover the rocks, they can never stray far from the sea. However, adventurous crabs climbing higher up the shore may find themselves scrambling not over rock but over the rough, horny skin of a basking iguana. Like barber-fish (page 10) and oxpeckers (page 12), the crabs forage for ticks and other bloodsucking parasites that live in the scaly crevices of their hosts – much to the benefit of the iguanas, which cannot always scratch their parasites away.

Large blue butterflies and ants

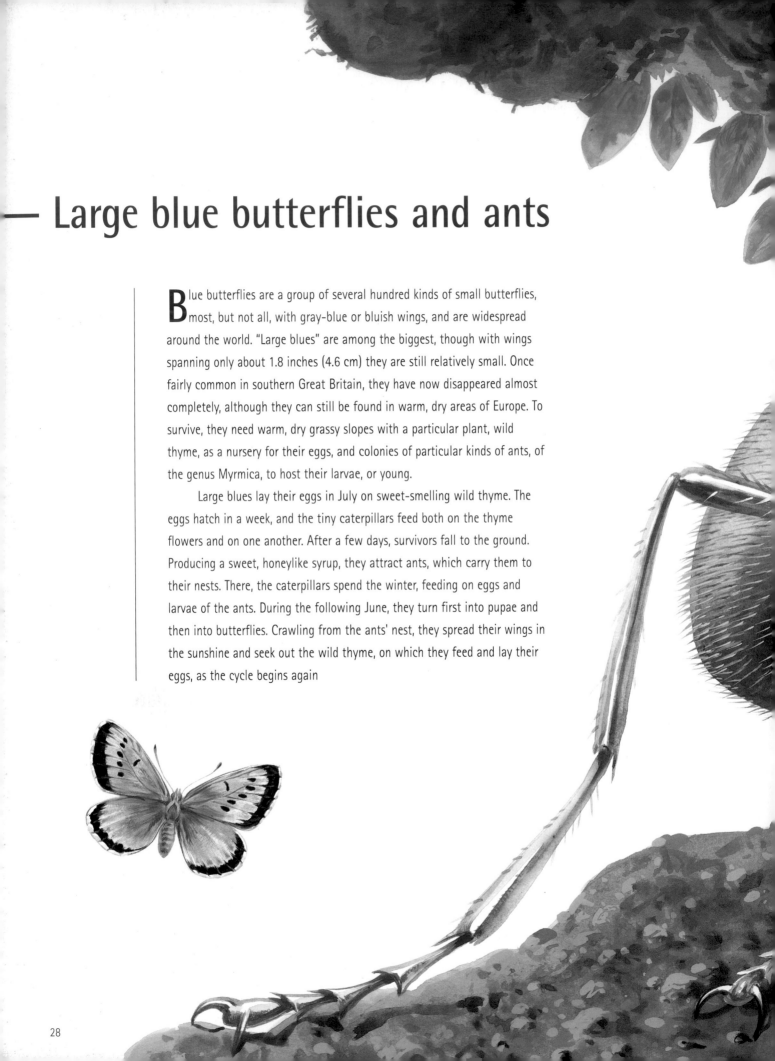

Blue butterflies are a group of several hundred kinds of small butterflies, most, but not all, with gray-blue or bluish wings, and are widespread around the world. "Large blues" are among the biggest, though with wings spanning only about 1.8 inches (4.6 cm) they are still relatively small. Once fairly common in southern Great Britain, they have now disappeared almost completely, although they can still be found in warm, dry areas of Europe. To survive, they need warm, dry grassy slopes with a particular plant, wild thyme, as a nursery for their eggs, and colonies of particular kinds of ants, of the genus Myrmica, to host their larvae, or young.

Large blues lay their eggs in July on sweet-smelling wild thyme. The eggs hatch in a week, and the tiny caterpillars feed both on the thyme flowers and on one another. After a few days, survivors fall to the ground. Producing a sweet, honeylike syrup, they attract ants, which carry them to their nests. There, the caterpillars spend the winter, feeding on eggs and larvae of the ants. During the following June, they turn first into pupae and then into butterflies. Crawling from the ants' nest, they spread their wings in the sunshine and seek out the wild thyme, on which they feed and lay their eggs, as the cycle begins again

Carmine bee-eaters and Kori bustards

Bustards are heavy, turkeylike birds, the biggest weighing over 30 pounds (13.5 kg), with wings spanning 7 feet (2 m) or more. Despite their weight they can fly well. Some that nest in western Europe make long migratory flights to eastern Asia. When nesting they spend much of their time on the ground, scratching with powerful claws looking for insects. This puts them in danger of ground predators, including people. Once plentiful throughout Europe, Africa, and Asia, sadly they are becoming rarer. They nest on the ground, each pair raising three or four chicks, which the mother bustard occasionally carries on her back.

Kori bustards, among the biggest of the family, live on the dry plains and scrublands of eastern Africa. Here, they share their range with carmine bee-eaters, some of the world's most elegant and gorgeously colored birds. Bee-eaters not only eat bees, but all kinds of small flying insects, many of which they catch on the wing, usually in short flights from a perch. Kori bustards and bee-eaters form an unlikely partnership. The bustard goes about its business, walking and scratching, with three or four bee-eaters riding on its back. Winged insects disturbed from the vegetation fly upward, and the bee-eaters make short forays to catch them in flight.

Egyptian coursers and Nile crocodiles

Travelers in Egypt many centuries ago reported that Nile crocodiles, though well known to be fierce, miraculously opened their jaws to allow a certain kind of bird to enter and pick meat from their teeth. Later, writers dismissed this as legend, until it was shown to be true.

The birds in question are Egyptian coursers. They are ploverlike birds with long legs. They nest on the ground and, although they can fly perfectly well, they run or crouch to escape danger. Living in tropical countries, usually near rivers or lakes, they feed mainly on insects, shellfish, lizards, and other small ground-dwelling animals. To this day, you can see them picking fragments of meat, together with leeches and other parasites, from crocodiles' mouths.

Cleaning crocodiles' teeth is just one of many tricks known to Egyptian coursers. Nesting on open beaches in the hot tropical sunshine, they are in constant danger of overheating, and so are their eggs and chicks. During the hottest weather they incubate only at night, when air temperatures fall dramatically. In the daytime, the mother bird buries the eggs, and later the chicks, under a layer of sand, cooling the sand by bringing water from the river in her crop, and throwing it up over the nest site.

Gray hornbills and green monkeys

Hornbills are birds of African and Asian forests. Though those bills look heavy, they are hollow and quite light – useful for poking into bushes, and delicate enough to pick up small berries and insects. Gray hornbills, up to 2 feet (60 cm) long, are less colorful than many of their kind. They live in the savanna, the sparse forest that covers huge areas of central and southern Africa. When they are around, you hear their honking alarm calls before you see them.

Gray hornbills share the forest with bands of monkeys, including the green monkeys, or vervets, shown here. "Green" is an exaggeration – they are usually yellowish-brown, with dark brown faces and white throats. They live in bands of a dozen or more, which gather close together to roost in the treetops at night but spread out to forage during the day. Their food is mainly leaves and fruits, gathered from the trees or the forest floor.

A band of monkeys moving through the lower forest branches creates quite a disturbance, stirring the foliage and dislodging insects and other small animals. These are what gray hornbills like to eat, so the hornbills have learned to watch out for the monkeys and follow them. In return, the hornbills give loud alarm calls that alert the monkeys to danger.

— Pea-crabs and blue mussels

Crabs come in all sizes, from tiny to enormous. Here is one of the smallest. The size of a pea, it lives in the shell of a living mussel, which in turn lives on a muddy seashore somewhere along the coast of Europe. With a shell less than half an inch (1.3 cm) across, this pea-crab is a fully grown female.

Like any other kind of crab, it started life as an egg, which floated to the surface of the sea and turned into a tiny, free-swimming larva. After several months and several changes in shape, it settled on a bank of mussels and found its way into one of the shells. There, it finally changed into a tiny crab, growing, maturing, and eventually producing eggs of its own.

The mussel makes a living by pulling in seawater through its gills, and filtering out tiny fragments of plant and animal life, which pass into its stomach and are digested. The crab runs over the mussel's gills, cleaning off some of the fragments for itself. It leads a quiet life, so doesn't need a lot of food. And the mussel seems none the worse for having a pea-crab wandering around in its shell.

Cattle egrets and cape buffaloes

Egrets are long-legged birds related to herons. They are usually white, with long yellow bills and fluffy plumes on their head and neck. Cattle egrets stand about 2 feet (60 cm) tall. They like company – where there is one, there are usually several dozen. Above all, they like to be with cattle, wild or tame. If there are no cattle, they will settle for horses, zebras, antelopes, or even elephants.

These cattle egrets have found a herd of cape buffaloes, and are poking around in the grass among their legs. Most egrets live in wetlands, feeding on fish, frogs, and other aquatic animals. Cattle egrets prefer dry grasslands, and feed mainly on the insects to be found there, especially grasshoppers, crickets, beetles, and other flying or hopping insects. Cattle attract flies, and stir up other insects as they move through the grasslands. Cattle egrets benefit from this, catching more insects when they are close to a herd than when they are on their own.

Though you usually see cattle egrets walking or perching, they fly strongly and are great travelers. Three hundred years ago they were found only in Africa and Asia. Now they have spread to North and South America, Australia, and even remote New Zealand, wherever people have taken their herds of domestic cattle.

Shrimp fish and sea urchins

Of all the world's animals, fish are the most remarkable for their strange shapes and ways of life. Here is a shrimp fish, one of the strangest. Four different kinds are known, and possibly there are more. They are related to seahorses and pipefish, and live in shallow coastal waters of the Indian and Pacific oceans. The biggest are about 1 foot (30 cm) long.

Shrimp fish do not look at all like shrimp. The only similarity is a transparent bony covering, like a thin shell. Seen from the side, they are slender and tapering, with a long tubular mouth, a long colored body, and a long spiny tail. Seen from below, they are almost transparent. When a shrimp fish stands upright in the water and turns its stomach toward you, it becomes almost invisible.

If a long thin fish needs to hide, where does it go? Some stand on their head among long, narrow strands of seaweed or sea grass, others among strands of horny coral. These shrimp fish have found a sea urchin with spines similar in color and shape to themselves and have dived down among them. First, a predator has to spot one among those movable and sharply pointed spines, then try to extract it, and neither will be easy.

Shepherd fish and Portuguese men-of-war

Man-of-war is an old-fashioned name for a battleship under sail. "Portuguese man-of-war" is an old sailors' name for particular kinds of jellyfish with gas-filled bladders, up to 4 inches (10 cm) long, that catch the wind like sails. They are found in warm and temperate oceans, often dozens together like fleets of tiny sailing ships. The bladders and underlying jelly may be blue, purple, or yellow-brown. These jellyfish look very beautiful and harmless. But if you see one, keep away – they can be deadly, even to humans.

Beneath each bladder hang strands of tentacles up to 30 feet (9 m) long, armed with stinging cells, and thousands of tiny mouths. As the jellyfish sails through the water, small animals get caught up in its tentacles, and are stung to death with a poison as powerful as snake venom. Then the tentacles draw the prey upward toward the mouths, which digest them.

Despite all this, one or two small fish, called shepherd fish, are often found living below the jelly. They dart in and out among the tentacles and seem quite unaffected by the stings. How do they manage this? We do not know, but these little fish have found as safe a haven from predators as anywhere else in the sea.

Black garden ants and rose aphids

Ants of all kinds will travel far to find sugary liquids. Here are some that have climbed the thorny stalks of a rose bush to find a source in the bodies of rose aphids.

Aphids are tiny, soft-bodied insects of different colors. Gardeners call the green ones greenfly. They feed on plants, particularly on the soft cells of new buds, sucking out juices that are rich in sugars, proteins, and minerals. They breed quickly, so often several hundred of them cluster on a single bud or young stem. To gain enough proteins and minerals, they have to take in more sugars than they need. So they excrete the surplus sweetness in a liquid called "honeydew." On rose bushes in spring, you often see lower leaves varnished and sticky with honeydew, a sure sign that thousands of aphids are at work higher up.

Black garden ants on the ground below sense the honeydew and climb up the rose stems to find its source – the aphids themselves. They caress these to obtain fresh honeydew, which they carry back to the nest in their stomachs. Like farmers looking after their herds, they protect the aphids from attack by other insects, squirting predatory lacewings and ladybird larvae with jets of stinging formic acid.

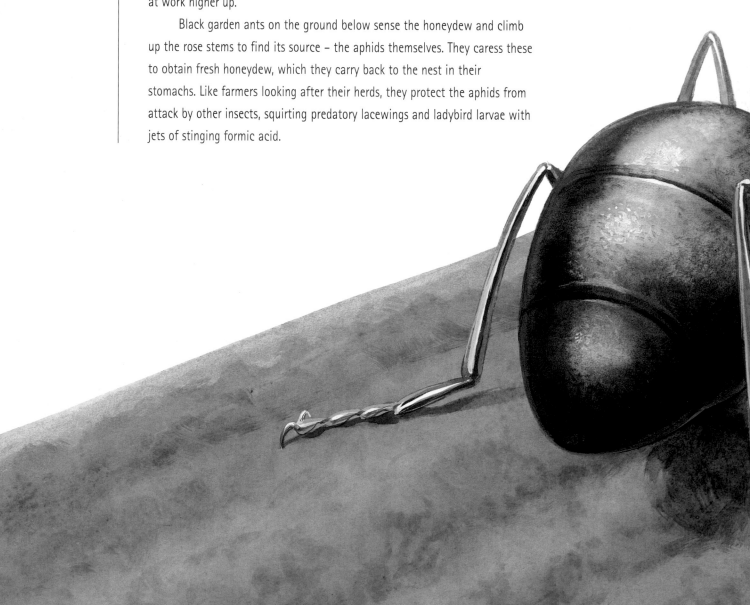

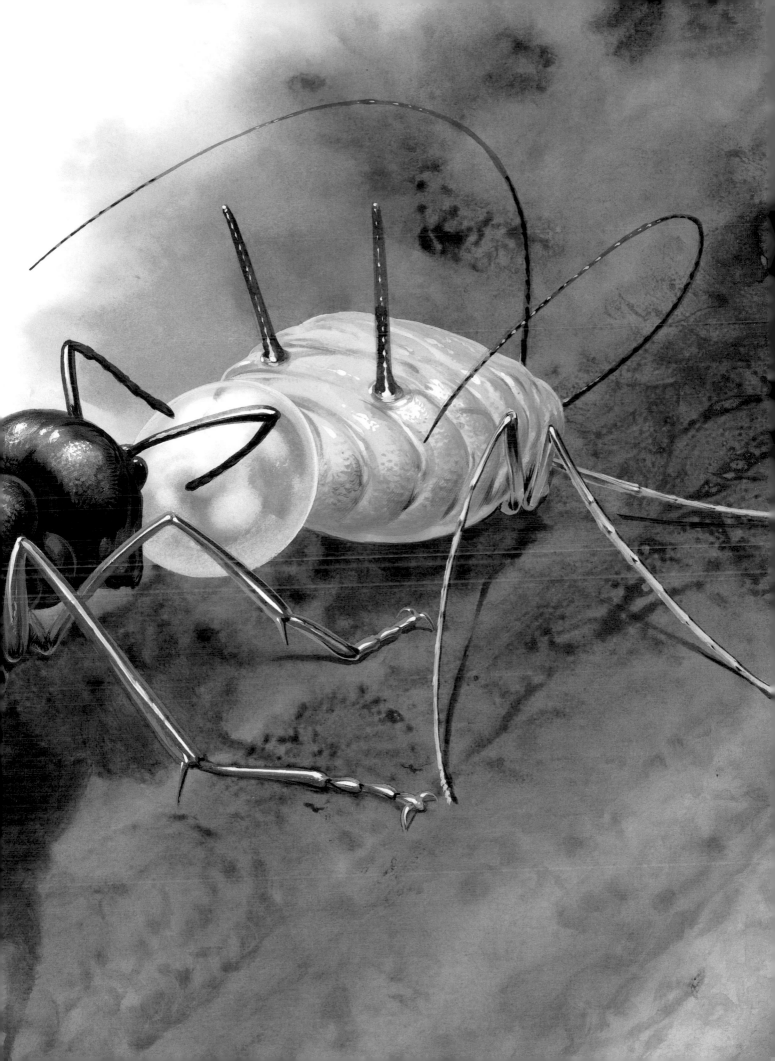

Black-capped chickadees and humans

Titmice and chickadees are small birds 4–5 inches (10–12.7 cm) long. They are often brightly patterned with black, gray, or blue on top, yellow or buff underneath. Britons who put out winter food for birds become familiar with various kinds of titmice. Americans have a very near look-alike, black-capped chickadees. These are all closely related birds of temperate woodlands, with similar habits of feeding and breeding, which have taken readily to life with people.

They nest in holes, often found in old trees, cliffs, or banks. In gardens and managed forests, there are often more breeding pairs than suitable holes, so they take readily to nest boxes provided by humans. Under natural conditions they feed on nuts and seeds throughout winter, switching to insects, particularly small caterpillars and aphids, when they are feeding their growing chicks in summer.

Titmice and chickadees quickly learn to take food from bird feeders. By putting out strings of peanuts, half coconuts, and mixed-seed feeders, we help them through the difficult winter months. In particularly hard years, we may save them from starvation, or at least from having to make long trips in search of food, and help them to start breeding in good time when spring comes around.

Index CREATURES AND FEATURES

A
Africa 8, 12, 14, 30, 34, 38
ant 28, 44
antelope 6, 8, 12, 38
aphid 44, 46
Asia 14, 30, 34, 38
Australia 18, 22, 38

B
badger 6, 14
barber-fish 10, 26
bee 6, 14
bee-eater 30
beetle 16, 38
black-capped chickadee 46
black garden ant 44
buffalo 38
burrow 18
bustard 30
butterfly 28

C
cape buffalo 38
caterpillar 28, 46
cattle 38
cattle egret 38
cheetah 8
chickadee 46
cleaner-wrasse 10
cod 10
coral 10, 40
coral cod 10
courser 32
crab 6, 10, 26, 36
crocodile 32

D
deer 6

E
egg 18, 20, 22, 28, 32, 36
egret 38
Egypt 32

Egyptian courser 32
elephant 8, 38
Europe 28, 30, 36

F
false scorpion 16
fish 6, 10, 20, 24, 40, 42
fish-hawk 20
flies 38

G
Galápagos Islands 26
Galápagos red crab 26
giraffe 8
Great Britain 28
great white shark 24
green monkey 34
greenfly 44
gull 6, 20

H
heron 20, 38
honey badger 6, 14
honeybee 14
honeydew 44
honeyguide 6, 14
hornbill 34
horse 38
host 6, 12, 24, 26, 28
human 16, 42, 46
hyena 8

I
iguana 26
Indian Ocean 40

J
jellyfish 42

K
kingfisher 22
kookaburra 22
Kori bustard 30

L
lacewing 44
ladybird larvae 44
large blue butterfly 28
larva 14, 16, 28, 36, 44
lion 6, 8
lizard 18, 26

M
man-of-war 42
mite 16
monkey 34
mussel 6, 36

N
nectar 14
New Zealand 18, 38
night-heron 20
Nile crocodile 32
North America 38

O
osprey 20
ostrich 6, 8
ox 12
oxpecker 6, 12, 26

P
Pacific Ocean 40
parasite 10, 12, 16, 26, 32
pea-crab 6, 36
penguin 26
perch 24
pipefish 40
poison 42
pollen 16
Portuguese man-of-war 42
predator 6, 8, 10, 14, 20, 22, 24,
   30, 40
prey 20
pseudoscorpion 16
pupae 28

R
ratel 14
remora 24
rhinoceros 12
rufous kookaburra 22

S
savanna 34
scorpion 16
sea urchin 40
seahorse 40
seaweed 20, 26, 40
shark 24
shearwater 18
shepherd fish 6, 42
shrimp 40
shrimp fish 40
snake 14, 22
sooty shearwater 18
South America 26, 38
starling 12

T
tentacle 42
termite 22
titmouse 46
tortoise 26
tuatara 18

V
vervet 34

W
wetlands 38
white shark 24
wild thyme 28
wrasse 10

Z
zebra 6, 8, 38